THE

GHOSTLY TALES

OF

OCALA
NATIONAL
FOREST

Published by Arcadia Children's Books
A Division of Arcadia Publishing, Inc.
Charleston, SC
www.arcadiapublishing.com

Spooky America is a trademark of Arcadia Publishing, Inc.

First published 2024
Manufactured in the United States

Designed by Jessica Nevins
Images used courtesy of Shutterstock.com; p. 28 Sunshower Shots/Shutterstock.com.

ISBN: 978-1-4671-9758-8
Library of Congress Control Number: 2024930947

Notice: The information in this book is true and complete to the best of our knowledge. It is offered without guarantee on the part of the author or Arcadia Publishing. The author and Arcadia Publishing disclaim all liability in connection with the use of this book.

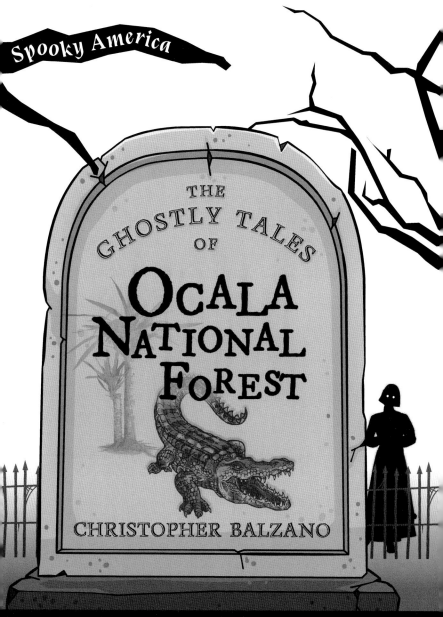

Spooky America

THE
GHOSTLY TALES
OF
OCALA
NATIONAL
FOREST

CHRISTOPHER BALZANO

Adapted from Haunted Ocala National Forest by Christopher Balzano

arcadia
CHILDREN'S BOOKS

GEORGIA

FLORIDA

ATLANTIC OCEAN

10

7

9

4   3   8   2

1   6

5

GULF OF MEXICO

• ORLANDO

TABLE OF CONTENTS & MAP KEY

Welcome to Spooky Ocala National Forest!

Take a look at spooky television shows, or horror movies, or the most popular YouTube channels. What do you see? Vampires and zombies. Ghosts causing jump scares, and shadows moving closer and closer. Lights turning on and off when no one is there. Voices in the dark. Glowing eyes watching you. Now, imagine all of these things happening in *one* place.

For millions of people around the world, Central Florida is known as the "happiest place on earth." But just an hour's drive from Orlando, the home of the magical and beloved Disney World theme parks, you'll find a vast and swampy woodland known for its evil spirits, mysterious ghosts, and even monsters.

Welcome to the Ocala National Forest. A place where nightmares come true.

Since Florida became a state back in 1845, people have been telling scary stories about its trees and swamps. After all, odd things find their way into these woods. People whisper about the ghost animals. About the balls of ghostly light and dark phantoms. There are even cemeteries that come alive at night.

But something else is different in the woods. A pond there one day disappears the next. An old cemetery on a trail sometimes moves to the other side of the road. Wait ... you know it was someplace else last week. People call it the Ocala Shift. If you live near here, you get used to it.

It's not just the national forest. People in the surrounding towns tell the same kinds of legends. When one ghost story sticks, you might call it cute. You hear it on Halloween and forget it by Thanksgiving. But when the stories keep coming from the same area, you know something is unique. You know something unexplained is going on. The line between creepy folklore and true tale of terror gets blurred.

Welcome to the blurred line.

Read this book with the lights on. Check to make sure the events in the chapter you're reading didn't occur too close to your house. Pretend you have never heard of the places mentioned. Keep telling yourself this is just a scary book that ends when you stop reading. There's nothing outside your window. There's nothing on that dark road on the edge of town. And there's absolutely, positively nothing in the woods. *Right?*

CHAPTER 1

The Curse of the Coyote Woman

PAISLEY

"Remember, Taylor. Never go near that cemetery at night."

"I remember, Grandpa. Never."

"And why don't we go there?"

"Because the Boogeyman lives there." Taylor stifled a laugh. He knew that was just a made-up story. He knew who roamed the cemetery at night. She was no Boogeyman.

Taylor's grandfather stopped and looked at

him, annoyed. They had walked this trail many times. Each time, the older man would tell the story as they wandered among the headstones. They would clean off any leaves or mud. It was their way of respecting the graves of the people who had lived in the town.

"It's not funny, Taylor. You laugh now, but you won't think it's funny if she takes you away."

But Taylor knew the story. He had been hearing it ever since he was five. His grandfather would point out the different parts of the forest as they walked from their house in Paisley to Lake Dorr. Whenever they came to the cemetery, they would stop. The tale would start, and Taylor would listen.

In this part of the woods, men knew to never come alone. There was a strange beast that appeared near the cemetery. It would come out of nowhere and take men not pure of heart. The men were never seen again.

The crying of the Coyote Woman would be heard for three days after.

She hadn't always been a beast. Sarah had been born to a loving mother and a strict father. She followed her family's rules. As she got older, people in the town talked about how beautiful she was. Her father kept a watchful eye on her. There was no one in town good enough for his daughter. But she had met a young man named Jake. He was nice to her. When no one was looking, he would slip her little presents. Her father disapproved. He caught Jake giving Sarah a flower one day. He refused to allow them to see each other again.

That didn't stop them, though. Sarah and Jake would sneak out and meet at the nearby cemetery in the woods. They knew no one else would come in after dark. They would talk until just before sunrise. Then they would each sneak home before anyone knew they had left.

That is, until Sarah's father caught his daughter coming back in through her window early one morning. He stormed into town and found Jake. There on Main Street, the father began to beat Jake in front of the whole town. No on tried to help. In fact, they cheered him on. The father then dragged Jake into the woods. Some say he killed Jake and buried him near the cemetery. Others say the young man got the message and moved to another town. Either way, he was never seen again.

Sarah heard what had happened. She went into town to find Jake. Everyone in town seemed to be staring at her.

"Why did none of you help him?" she yelled. They could not look her in the eyes. Some even laughed at her. Sarah cursed the men. She would get revenge on the wicked people of the town. She ran home and packed all her belongings. She was going to run away from this horrible place and never return.

Carrying everything she owned, she trekked to the cemetery. She would say goodbye to Jake in the only way she could. The sun was setting in the forest. As she stood next to the headstones, she began to cry. A pack of coyotes started to circle the cemetery. She lay down on the ground, crying harder and harder. The pack circled faster and faster. They began to howl loudly. Sarah was now so sad and angry, she was screaming. The sound of her voice began to mix with the coyotes. You could not tell one from the other. Her body began to change. Fur grew all over her, and her nose started to get longer. She sprang from the cemetery with the body of a coyote. She joined the pack.

"But that's not the end of the story, right Taylor?"

"No, Grandpa." Taylor had believed the story  when he was little. Now as a teenager, he thought it was silly. The weird howling they heard in the woods could be explained. Maybe it was a sick coyote. Maybe it was just another animal. He had never seen the woman. He and his friends had heard her cries often. He could not tell his grandfather the truth. They had made a game out of her story.

"The Coyote Woman is still out here. Her curse is still alive, Taylor."

During the day, people still see a beautiful woman looking at them from behind the trees. She is frowning. If they try to talk to her, she disappears. They chase after her but can never catch her.

Some nights, the voice of the pack is different than the others in the area. It sounds like a woman is crying and screaming with them. There are a lot of men who disappear in this part of the woods. People always whisper about how bad the men were. The weird shrieks of the pack are always heard around three days after these men disappear.

Taylor's friends had heard the story, too.

It scared them, but they would not admit it to each other. Instead, they'd made a game out of it. They would wait until everyone was asleep, and then go to the cemetery. By now, there was a fence surrounding it. They would lie on the ground, lay their arms across their chests, and chant the lovers' names. *Sarah, Jake. Sarah, Jake.* More than once, when they did this, they

heard the coyote's howl. The coyotes could be heard circling the cemetery. There would be an unusual voice with them, like a woman crying. The kids kept chanting. The crying would become a scream. The trick was to be the last one in the cemetery after everyone else ran away shouting.

Taylor never won.

CHAPTER 2

The Wanderer

ASTOR

No one can tell you exactly what the Wanderer looks like. He walks out of the woods and stalks the streets of Astor under the light of the moon. He strolls the roads, seen only in headlights. The Wanderer can appear anywhere. Every story about him is a little different.

"I've seen him," says a younger man, who looks around to make sure no one else is listening. "But I *hear* him more. I live over by the trailers on Gobbler Road. He bangs on our doors and then runs away. Don't laugh at me. I know it's not kids. How? Because when he runs away, he doesn't turn a corner or nothing. Poof. He's just gone."

"I have always seen him on Railroad Grade Road," says one older woman. "He is a tall man wearing a dark coat. You can see he has a face, but his head is down. I've seen him at least a dozen times. Right after I hear that train whistle."

This woman believes that the mysterious stranger worked the railroad. It used to run through Astor to deliver local wine to other parts of the state. Sometimes it carried passengers, too. One night, there was an accident. No one in town can quite say what happened. Newspapers didn't cover the event. But everyone in town believes the accident occured.

All the passengers lost their lives. Some were never found. The whistle of the ghost train can be heard when there's a full moon. Some believe the missing people might be walking the town, hoping someone has found their bodies.

"I see him near the bridge," says an older gentleman. "He walks across it and then stops. I'm not saying he is a shadow. He's just not all there. He goes to the middle of the bridge and raises his foot as if he is going to take a step. Then he disappears. He can't go into the next county."

About a hundred years ago, a drawbridge was built over the St. Johns River. It separates Lake County and Volusia County. One side of the bridge belongs to each county, but the line between the two is unclear. McQueen Johnson, the first man to operate the drawbridge, was murdered at work and his body was placed on the line dividing the two counties. No one wanted to take responsibility for investigating. The two counties argued, but the murder was never solved. It's said Johnson's spirit will walk the town of Astor until his murder is solved.

Some in town say he is the Wanderer.

"Yeah, I've seen the Wanderer a few times, always on State Road 40," says another man who has lived in Astor his whole life. "It's not like they say online. He's not a shadow. It's more like he's just not quite there. He's solid sometimes. You can even see he's wearing a cloak or something. It's all around him so it looks like he's just a dark figure. But I've seen his face. Big beard, dark eyes. A fog surrounds him. I know the Wanderer is the Monk. They should have never killed him."

In the town's early days, the people who lived on the St. John's River were French. They got along with the Timucua people who lived there. Then the Spanish moved down the river. They fought the French and anyone who was friends with them. They destroyed their settlements and villages. The Spanish set up a monastery where the French used to live. The Timucua wanted revenge. They snuck into the monastery at night. They killed all the monks except their leader. They burned the church to the ground and brought the head monk into what is now Astor. They hung him from a tree in the town center so the Spanish would know to stay away.

But the day after the hanging, the Monk's body was not there. Someone must have cut him down, they thought. That night, a thick fog rolled in. The Monk was seen walking through it. He took away two men as they screamed. The next night, the same thing happened. The Timucua knew something had to be done. They demanded their chief confront the Monk. The third night, the fog rolled in again, and the chief went out to meet him. No sound was heard. The next morning, they found the chief dead under the same tree. There was no damage to his body. He had died of fright.

Maybe the Monk is the man who walks Astor.

"Everybody else is wrong," says an old man with a fishing pole. He sits on the dock near an old motel and lets his feet dangle near the water. "No one has ever cleared the land on the Morrison Island. They are not allowed to. Chief Okahumpka won't let anybody live on his land, even though he must have died 200 years ago."

The old man continues. "You can tell it's Chief Okie by the footprints. On his way down here, he was attacked by a gator who got two of his toes. No one knows where he came from. He has never talked to anyone. He just walks down the street carrying a large pole with a big old hawk on the top of it. He floats over to Morrison Island on that thing. I've seen those footprints on the sand over there and left in mud over here. Of course, I've seen him on guard duty, too."

It's said that after Chief Okie set up camp on Morrison Island, he would not allow anyone else to cross the water to it. Several people came to town looking to settle the island. There are historical records of scouting parties going in. No one came out.

No one ever heard so much as a scream. They just crossed the water and disappeared into the woods. All people could hear was the loud cry of a hawk. They stopped sending people over.

"Every night he comes out," the old man continues. "I don't always see him, but he comes out. That guy is either a ghost or over 150 years old. I'll let you decide. Many nights, sometime just after 10:00 p.m., a shadow man comes from the woods to the edge of the water. He looks around and then floats back into the woods. Chief Okie is looking after his island.

"We've settled much of this area. I don't think he likes it. I think he's walking around, mad at what we've done around here. We might have the town, but he has that island."

The old man finishes and turns to look back toward the island.

Maybe the Wanderer is all of them. There

is just too much history in Astor, too many ghosts of things gone wrong. The people of Astor know to stay out of the ghosts' way. They know they own the town by day. The Wanderer owns it at night.

Fort King, Ocala

CHAPTER 3

The Many Ghosts of Fort King

Kevin was excited when he pulled into Fort King. He had been driving through Ocala when he saw a reenactment happening there. At least a dozen people were walking around the front lawn. They were wearing old-fashioned clothes. Some were gathered around a fire. Some were marching. Some were even holding guns. Kevin thought they were ready to share stories.

Kevin was surprised more cars were not parked in the lot. He stopped the first ranger he saw. "Is there a cost for the event?"

"Event?" The ranger gave Kevin an odd look. "We are not having an event today." But deep down, he knew what was going on. This kind of thing had happened before. Kevin had seen the ghosts.

Fort King was originally built in 1827. It was erected to help protect the Seminole Indian Agency across the street. The original purpose of the SIA was to help with problems between the Seminoles and the Floridians who lived in the area. As tensions between those two groups got stronger, the government wanted army protection.

In 1835, famous Seminole leader Osceola killed army officer Wiley Thompson and then attacked Fort King. This sparked the Second Seminole War, which lasted from 1835 until

1842. Since then, people have seen ghosts at Fort King. Visitors driving by see men walking on the front lawn, holding guns and dressed in old-fashioned clothes. They pull in, thinking it's a special event. Kids attending summer camp at the fort talk about unseen hands that throw their balls while they play. When they chase the ball, it only rolls away again. The rangers talk about seeing several different men with long beards in the towers. They shout to the men to get down. They go up to investigate, but no one is there.

Many soldiers were buried in front of the fort. They may have been laid to rest, but it didn't last. They were dug up and moved. Most were reburied almost a hundred miles away in St. Augustine. Perhaps the men are looking for their graves.

They are confused and can't find peace. They wander around searching. They walk over to the welcome center and bang on the doors. People who work at Fort King say it happens all the time.

"I was working one day, the whole building shook suddenly. I thought a tree had fallen." Candice has heard her share of strange things there. "I went out, and there was nothing there. I heard crying, though."

The fort that stands today is new. Over the last 200 years, it has burned down several times. It is always rebuilt. Maybe the ghosts are confused, looking for the garrison they knew. This is common for ghosts. They get angry when the place they once knew changes.

People in the neighborhood around Fort King think the soldiers don't stay put.

Sometimes, they are seen in nearby houses. Kids wake up to find a man holding a gun trying to talk to them. When they scream, the men disappear.

Then there are the ghosts of the two lovers. Long before Fort King was built, the indigenous peoples of the area used a spring located in the back of the fort. This was even before the Seminoles settled in Ocala. There was something magical about the spring. According to a well-known story, those who drink from the spring will have good health and a long life. The local indigenous peoples even buried their honored dead nearby. They believed the spring would protect them.

A Seminole woman used to get water for her family from the spring. She knew it was dangerous. The United States government and the Seminoles were at war with each other. The special water was important, though.

One day, she met a handsome soldier. Rather than try and capture her, he was nice. He offered to help her bring the water back to her family. Slowly, they fell in love. They would sneak out and meet by the spring. They talked about getting married after the war was over.

Soon, the solider was called into duty. He was part of a troop that would go out at night and look for the Seminoles. One night, the Seminoles were alerted that the soldiers were coming. They ambushed the troop and killed all the soldiers. When the woman found out, she was struck with grief. She went to the spring and prayed for her beloved. Some soldiers thought she had come to attack Fort King. They shot and killed her. Rather than bury the woman, they tossed her body into the water. They laughed at what they had done.

The man she loved had not died, though. He was wounded and brought back to the base. He heard about the woman who had been killed and went down to see her. He tried to get her out of the water, but the other men would not let him. A fight broke out. The man was accidentally shot and died.

To this day, the two lovers still find each other. Every December and January, people know not to go down to the spring. There is not much to see there anyway. Now it looks like a dirty pond covered with green algae. People no longer drink the water. Animals no longer gather there.

In fact, no one uses the spring but the two ghosts who meet there to try and relive their love. On certain nights, a low fog covers all of Fort King. Some have reported seeing two ghostly figures appear on different sides of the pond. People can't tell you exactly who they

are. At first, two two ghosts glow bright green. Then, they transform into balls of light. Each is about the size of a basketball. They slowly float over the water toward each other. Finally, they join in the middle above the old spring, splash into the water, and disappear.

The Haunted Road

DUNNELLON

Most people like a good horror movie. Everybody has their favorites. Part of the fun is that the movie ends. You can shut it off and go back to your normal life. It's just a movie, after all. There is no reason to be scared. But what if it didn't end? What if scary things still happened in the place where the movie was made? In Ocala National Forest, you just might find the horror movie is still playing.

Tiger Trail Road in Dunnellon is pretty famous. If you are a horror movie fan, you might even recognize it. It's where the movie *Jeepers Creepers* was shot in 2001. Some people say the movie cursed the area somehow. Other say the filmmakers chose the area because they believed it was haunted. It's a straight road with trees that look like people with outstretched arms. Even by sunlight,

something is creepy about it. The road leads to the local high school. They call it Tiger Tail Road because the school's mascot is a tiger. At night, however, the road becomes something different. The school is dark, and there are no streetlights. The trees look like monsters trying to reach down to the road. But *they* are not what you should fear. Because if you walk Tiger Tail Road at night, there is a good chance you may see a ghost. There is also a chance you may come across something even creepier.

Balls of light known as orbs float in the middle of the street. They appear in different sizes and different colors. Some are orange and some are white or red. If you are driving down the road, you may mistake them for people looking for a ride. The orbs drift in the air and wait. Drivers slow down, and the orbs fly toward them before floating higher in the air.

When the drivers look again, the orbs have vanished.

But drivers also see children in the road. They say they are younger than teenagers, but not by much. The children are wearing normal clothes and sneakers and look like average tweens. Sometimes they are standing in the street and other times they are dancing and waving hello right on the edge of it. Kids should not be out that late, the drivers think, and they stop.

That's when they notice the children have creepy smiles and black eyes. The children tap or gently knock on the windows, still grinning. Sometimes, the "Black-Eyed Kids" even ask to be let into the cars. You should *never* let them in. These children are not what they appear to be. No one knows quite what they are, but it's clear they are something inhuman. They are said to knock on peoples' doors late at night, crying and asking for help. Just like on the road, the children look human—except for their eyes. Some locals say they are more like vampires. But like vampires, they can't come in ... unless you *invite* them.

As a rule, if you see an eerie kid by the side of the road who asks to get in your car, drive away as fast as you can! Some say, if you are driving at 3:00 a.m. on the road by yourself, two of the children will appear in your backseat. All they want is for you to talk to them. If this happens, just ignore them. They'll get annoyed and yell at you, but then they'll disappear.

Maybe the scariest ghost on Tiger Tail Road is the Dark Man. He may not be a ghost at all. He is all black with glowing red eyes. He wears a hat. Many describe him as looking like the bad guy from the movie *Jeepers Creepers*. People claim to have seen him many places around Ocala National Forest, but in Dunnellon, you can make him appear. Drive a little past the high school and turn off the car. Turn your lights on and off. When you turn them on again, you will see a dark figure in the distance. Turn them off, turn them on, and he'll be a little closer, staring at you with glowing eyes. He won't say a word, but you'll know he wants to come closer.

Do it again, and he'll be so close, you'll hear his heavy breathing.

Flash your lights on and off again, and he'll be close enough to put a hand on the hood of the car. Switch on the lights one more time. He'll appear in the car right beside you. No one ever says what happens then.

Usually, people get scared when they spot him on the road and want to speed away. This is a *bad* idea. He will follow you home. Instead, you must restart the car and turn on your high beams. Then, turn them on and off, and he will be a little farther away. Keep doing this until he is completely gone, as if maybe you had only imagined him.

Is the School or the Cemetery Haunted?

High school can be scary. It's the fear of the unknown. Will you get good grades? Will you like your teachers? Will you make the team or make friends? The idea of walking those halls could make your heart race with fear. Now imagine you're sharing those halls with a *ghost*.

Many schools claim to have a ghost in them. At Pine Ridge High School in Deltona, students don't need to make up ghost stories.

Their ghosts are real. Sure, teachers talk about shadows they see in the classrooms at night. Teens who stay at school after dark for practice say they hear footsteps when no one is there. But the *really* creepy ghost at Pine Ridge High is different. It talks to the whole school during the morning announcements.

Since the school was built in 1994, students have heard a ghostly voice over the intercom system. No one can explain the low whisper that plays over the intercom, echoing through the hallways and classrooms during the day. It is not a radio signal or anyone on the

microphone. It's just a low mumbling no one can quite make out. For thirty years, students and teachers have scratched their heads. The bells also go off at odd times. When they do, it doesn't sound like the usual bells that ring when classes begin and end. There is an echo to them, like they are coming from far away.

Years ago, as the rumor goes, a man got hurt while installing the elevator. As he was working on it, something terrible happened. The elevator crushed him. He called out in pain and waited for the ambulance. By the time it got there, though, he had died. Today, the elevator takes students and teachers to the second floor, but it opens and closes whenever it wants. Sometimes, the elevator refuses to open at all. Other times, it opens when no one has pushed the button. People riding in it occasionally hear the same whisper heard on the loud speaker. Some have even heard a voice asking for help. Again, they can't determine where the voice is coming from. They've even tried to fix it, but how can you fix something if you can't find anything wrong?

The man in the elevator does not explain everything, though. Is he the same man who walks the classrooms at night? He is said to be more solid than a shadow but not human. People who have been inside the school at night say the man sneaks into the classrooms and locker rooms. Thankfully, he does not try to hurt anyone. He just stares and then vanishes when people notice him. Occasionally, he knocks over books and equipment trying to get their attention. Some say he is six feet tall

while others say he is smaller, like a little kid. Are they all the same ghostly man? Or is it possible the school might have more than one ghost?

Here is the tricky thing, though. According to school records, there was never a man who died while installing the elevator. No one can find a name. No one can find an ambulance or hospital report. It's just a story people have spread over the years. Some believe the key to the ghost's identity might be *next door* to the school. After all, just past the teacher parking lot is a cemetery. A cemetery that is thought to be haunted.

Osteen Cemetery is hard to find unless you know it's there. It is hidden behind new houses and fences. You have to travel down a curvy road just to find it. It was started by the town founders, many of whom are buried there. Though cemeteries are thought to be peaceful, people say this one is not. They report a dark shadow, just like the one at the school. They hear footsteps behind them when no one is there. When they turn, they hear running but do not see anyone. They even hear a low whisper they can't understand. Here, you always feel like someone is watching you.

Then there's the Whistling Man. No one ever sees him, but plenty of people have heard him. It's said that he whistles a sad song. Maybe he is an old mourner, grieving the death of a loved one. Perhaps he is buried in the cemetery and whistling to make himself feel better.

Nobody knows for sure why the souls of Osteen Cemetery seem to be so restless. The

trouble could be that not all of the cemetery is there anymore. New houses cut into what used to be the cemetery grounds. The fences that were built to give residents privacy and block out the old headstones may have disturbed something. A strange fog, not seen anywhere else in the cemetery, floats by the fence. Where did those old headstones go? Some were made of wood or cheap stone. They may have been destroyed in storms or by the harsh Florida sun. Town records say they should be there, but none can be found.

Then there's the part of the cemetery no one talks about. A plaque donated to the cemetery tells its history. There is a brief mention of

an "African American graveyard to the west." Some of these graves belonged to local people who had been enslaved or died after the Civil War. Their cemetery has been destroyed. No one knows what happened to the headstones or the bodies. All that's known is that teachers park their cars west of the cemetery.

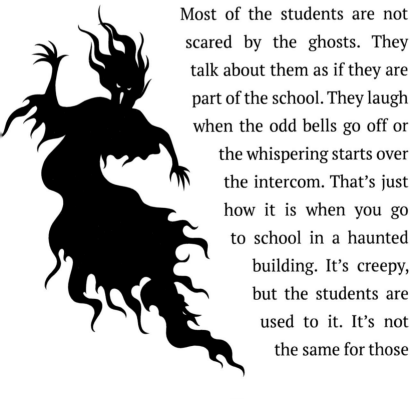

Most of the students are not scared by the ghosts. They talk about them as if they are part of the school. They laugh when the odd bells go off or the whispering starts over the intercom. That's just how it is when you go to school in a haunted building. It's creepy, but the students are used to it. It's not the same for those who stay when the sun goes down. They never get used to the man watching them or the little children running in the halls. For them, school is the kind of place you should leave when the bell rings.

6

Eloise's Bells

STETSON UNIVERSITY

The two candidates stood at the base of Hulley Tower. Both wanted the job of ringing Stetson University's famous bells. They were nervous. Only one could get the job. They had spent the last hour in the tower. The man interviewing them had given them a tour. He had shown them how the bells worked. He had gone over the tight schedule of when the bells had to be rung. He had even shown them where the two bodies were laid to rest in the base of the tower. There was just one more question to ask them.

"What do you think of Hulley Tower?" the interviewer asked the first candidate.

"It is beautiful. I can't wait to be part of a great tradition."

The interviewer hid his disappointment. He then asked the second man the same question.

"It's all a bit overwhelming," the man replied. "I have a question for you, though. Was it just me, or is there a strange wind up there? It almost sounded like someone was trying to talk to me."

The interviewer smiled. He knew who would get the job. Eloise Hulley had chosen the new bell ringer herself. It didn't matter that she had been dead for more than fifty years. She always knew the right person for the job.

The ghost of Eloise Hulley had been choosing who would ring her bells since her death in 1959. Her husband, Lincoln, had been one of the founders of Stetson. As they built the University, he wanted to do something special for his wife. She had always loved bells. He called for a tower to be built to celebrate her. Its bells would ring at the beginning of classes every morning and when classes were over. They would celebrate important moments at the college. Eloise would have her bells.

Lincoln died in 1934, just before the tower was completed. Though he never got to hear them, his wife cherished the bells until the day she died. The Stetson community loved them, too.

Hulley Tower became the center of the campus. People would meet up there before going to class. They would rub the base of it for good luck before a football game. It was said to help students on big tests. If you were nervous, you could visit the bell tower before class and lay your hands on it, saying the name of the class. You were promised at least a C.

When Eloise died, she and Lincoln were entombed in the base of the tower. This means anyone who entered the tower would walk right by their graves. It was tradition to say hello to them as you passed. If you didn't, the legend said you would trip on the stairs, or the bells wouldn't work. It was an honor to be the one who rang the bells. You were part of a long, important part of campus life. Eloise's ghost was said to whisper into the ear of the person she wanted to have the job. She might even tug on their shirt or pat them on the back. When a candidate reported these strange happenings, they got the job.

Eloise would pat the bell ringers on the back as they worked. She would race them up the stairs of the tower. Some said they'd feel the air suddenly turn cold and then a fast breeze would blow by them. Eloise loved to play games like that. It was her way of saying the bell ringer was moving too slow. A few times, her ghost rang the bells herself. For one reason or another, no one had shown up to do it. It did not matter. The bells still sounded through the campus. The next time the bell ringer showed up, they could not open the doors. They had to apologize before Eloise would let them in.

Hulley Tower was taken down in 2005. Over the years, the tower had become damaged. Officials thought someone might get hurt if the tower fell during a bad storm or hurricane. They removed Eloise's bells from the tower and split them up in different locations all around the campus. People wondered what would happen to Eloise's ghost. Would she stay now that her bells had been taken away?

It seems she and her husband like the spot. Sometimes the bells can be heard even though the tower is no longer there. This is said to happen on Eloise and Lincoln's anniversary.

Lincoln and Eloise were truly in love. Even after their deaths, the students and staff know just how strong that love is. They say the two often appear together just as the sun is coming up. Go to the former spot of Hulley Tower at dawn and you might see them yourself! They are walking hand in hand along the lawn, in front of the spot where their tower once stood. Sometimes, the dog Lincoln loved so much in life is with them. If you ever happen see Lincoln and Eloise, don't try to talk to them. They have everything they need. They have each other ... and the quiet sounds of the ghost bells.

The Stikini's Warning

OLD KING ROAD

You hear a noise outside your window and try to ignore it. You turn in your bed and place your pillow tight against your ears to block it out. It does not help. The noise is still there. A bit closer than before. You think hard, trying to place what it might be. That will make you feel better. It's only an owl, you tell yourself. It's a bird awake at night. They are spooky, but nothing to fear. You close your eyes and try to fall asleep. You think you are safe.

But that is because you do not know about the Stikini. They are witch vampire owls from Seminole folklore, and they live in Florida. If you live near Ocala National Forest, they live near you. They are outside your window or hunting in the woods.

In the daylight, the Stikini appear in the woods as beautiful women. They may lure men into the woods until they are lost. They then drink their blood. At night, they hunt in their true form. They are over six feet tall with an owl's head and wings. Sometimes, they are said to have human legs. They can fly to the top of the trees.

Legend says there was a Seminole woman who practiced magic. One day, some settlers who'd come to Florida killed her husband. In her pain and anger, she called on a special goddess named She Who Walks the Circle. The woman wanted the goddess's power to get revenge on her husband's murders. She found the settlers and killed them. When she was done, she did not want to give back the goddess's power. She began attacking other men, including Seminoles, who she felt treated women badly. With each spell she cast for power, the woman lost a little of who she was. Her body changed. Soon, she was no longer a woman but a Stikini.

Late 1835 was not a good time to be in Florida. The United States government had called for all Native Americans living in Florida to be moved west to Oklahoma. Some in the Seminole Nation had signed a treaty to do this.

Many felt those who had signed did not represent all the people. They refused to leave. As things got worse, Fort King in Ocala needed more soldiers for the coming war.

On December 23, 1835, 110 men left Fort Brooks in Tampa on their way to Fort King. The soldiers began their march down a road called King's Road. They were led by Major Francis Langhorne Dade. Over the next few days, the men found that getting across the land was not as easy as they had thought. Even today, this

part of Florida is covered with thick woods and swamps. But back then, the road was nothing more than a trail, barely large enough for the men and the equipment. Dangers were all around as they travelled the narrow path. Some Seminoles destroyed bridges along the way. The soldiers had a hard time moving their cannons across the water. Their weight caused them to sink in the wet, soggy land.

The troops were ambushed on December 28 in what is now Bushnell. The Seminoles had

been hiding in the swamps and behind the thick trees. The soldiers shot blindly into the woods and could not set up their cannons. When the smoked cleared, 107 of them had been killed and only three survived. Two escaped and ran to Fort King. One of them was caught and killed. Another man, James Sprague, fled back to Fort Brooks.

It was a great victory for the Seminoles, but it led to the Second Seminole War. This battle became known as the Dade Massacre. Many books have been written about the historical facts of this event.

But some Seminoles tell a different story. They whisper of the Stikini.

They say Sprague told a different story when he got back to the fort. On their first night out, two men disappeared. The next day, some soldiers saw beautiful women in the woods. They thought they were Seminole spies and tried to ignore them. That night, they heard screams and an owl screech coming from the trees. By morning, five more were gone. Again, the women walked with them through the swamp. The men said they could hear them whispering in their ears. Some left the road and went with the women and were never seen again.

That night, the shrieking owls grew louder. Major Dade had already lost almost thirty men. The soldiers formed circles with their guns raised. They would not be taken. Sprague was so scared, he ran into the woods and hid. All he could hear was the sound of the other soldiers screaming. He dared not look. He just pushed himself closer against the tree. When the sun came up, he began walking back to Fort Brooks. But he did not take the road. Instead, he walked slowly through the woods, trying not to make a sound.

Sprague walked all day until the sun went down. He wanted to sleep, but he was too scared. To stay awake, he sang an old song his mother had taught him. Then, her voice joined his. He could hear his mother singing in his ears. She appeared a short distance from him in the woods. She was smiling and moving her hand for him to follow her. He couldn't control himself. He followed. His mother vanished behind a tree. Still, he followed. He came upon a clearing in the trees and discovered a terrifying sight. Three Stikini stood with their backs to him. They were in front of a giant cauldron. The smell was sickening.

They must have sensed his presence because they turned and faced him. Sprague saw their owl faces and talons. He shook with fear. Then one of them spoke.

"Let them know what you have seen here," it said. The voice sounded like an owl's hoot, but there was just enough human sound that he understood. "Stay out of the woods," it warned. "Stay out of the swamp. *Stay out*."

After a few days, Sprague made it back to the fort and told the others what he had seen. He gave them the Stikini's warning. They did not follow it.

In the end, the Seminoles lost the war, and more people came to live near the Ocala National Forest. They settled all along what was once King's Road. There is no highway now, just smaller roads. There are off-road paths for jeeps and four-wheelers. During the day, people are fine. Sometimes, they see weird shadows in the woods. They feel they are being watched or even followed. Some say they see beautiful women. But the women fade away and disappear when anyone tries to talk to them.

At night, it is a different story. Sometimes, a car is going down the road and its engine will mysteriously stop. The driver then hears an owl screeching. The car shakes like something is trying to get in. Then the car turns on again. When the driver checks the car, there are talon scratches on the roof and doors.

Sometimes, people disappear in the area. Friends walking in the woods after dark will

hear a swoosh from the trees. Then one of their companions is gone.

So, if you hear an owl screeching outside at night, lock your windows. It might just be an owl getting ready to hunt. Or an owl talking to another owl. It might be something else, though. If you have broken the rules set by the Skitini about not walking in the woods, they might be giving you a warning.

Ghosts on the Water

Aunt Silla asked everyone to come closer. She was getting older, and it made it harder for her to speak loud enough for everyone in the crowd to hear. She had been telling the story longer than most of her family members had been alive.

"Long before Silver Springs Park was here, there was a handsome man named Clarice. He was the son of a rich man in the area. He fell in love with a woman named Bernice who worked for his father. I was friends with her. She was so stunning she could make the very waters stop flowing. But Clarice's father would not let them see each other. They would sneak out at night and row to a meeting point on the water."

At this, Aunt Silla would point slowly to the part of the water known as the Bridal Chamber. "Clarice's father found out about these secret visits and was as mad as an alligator. He sent Clarice far away so that the two could never meet again. Before he left, though, Clarice gave Bernice his mom's old gold bracelet. This was his way of promising that he would come back to her.

"I was the only friend Bernice had at the time. Clarice's father fired her, and she had nothing, so I took her in. She would not eat. She would not talk. She got weaker and weaker and sicker and sicker. One day, she asked me to row her out to the Bridal Chamber so she could see her favorite spot again. I thought maybe she'd see that water and it would bring life back to her. Didn't happen. She died on the way there, but not before she took my hand and begged me to lay her body in that water. I let her body fall over the side of the boat. I'm not lying when I say this. The bottom of the spring opened and *swallowed* her up.

"Clarice came home just a few days later. He came to this house right here to ask where his love was. I told him what I just told you. I took him out to the Bridal Chamber myself. He dove into that water. I watched him swimming deep, and then I saw a hand come out of nowhere. On the wrist, I saw that same gold bracelet. Clarice reached out for the hand, and it reached out for him. Then the bottom opened up again and they both disappeared.

"On moonlit nights, a ghost canoe travels

on those waters near the Bridal Chamber. It glows a dull white and disappears before it gets there. Spirits come to Silver Springs from all over to try and find their beloved lost loved ones. All around the Bridal Chamber, lights appear. They are the souls of the lovers. They wander the water, searching for those they've lost. Sometimes they find them. Sometimes they don't, but they come back time and again to keep looking."

In her lifetime, Aunt Silla saw Silver Springs Park become an international attraction. It was there before Disney and Busch Gardens and Universal Studios. Since the 1860s, people have been coming to the park to sail the springs and take in all the exhibits. It was the first

park to feature glass-bottom boats. People can peer down and see the wonders of the springs up close. Much of the land around the park remains wild and full of danger. Movies and television shows have been made there over the years, including *Tarzan* and *The Creature from the Black Lagoon*.

The people who work in the park know they may see a ghost at any time. Many who work at night see faces with no bodies floating in the windows. Music is sometimes heard from the ballroom the night before a wedding is held there. Some believe that if the ghost music plays, the marriage will last. Ghosts sometimes try to talk to guests, only to disappear right in front of them. The ghosts have been known to steal tools and move the food in the cafeteria. If the ghosts like you, they might help you out. Many of the employees say they can call out for a certain thing they can't find. When they turn around, the missing item is there. And all of them see the ghost lights on the water.

Today, many have forgotten Clarice and Bernice's story. But the spectral boat is still seen. Some say it belongs to Mourning Dove and Running Fox. The story goes that long ago, Indigenous peoples would come to Silver Springs to compete in games, sort of like the Olympics. One year, Running Fox came and won game after game. He could not be beat. He was walking near the water between races when he saw Mourning Dove. They fell in love at first sight. They would sit on the shore at a place known as the Twisted Palm and talk about a life together. Another man from the races, Brown Dog, hated Running Fox. He always came in second and loved Mourning Dove. He followed Running Fox until he was alone and killed him with a rock.

Mourning Dove rowed out to the Bridal

Chamber with Running Fox's body. At that time, the people in the area called it The Abyss. The people cried on the shore for the two lovers. By the time the canoe had reached The Abyss, Mourning Dove had vanished. Her body was never found.

Don't believe there's something to the story? A few years ago, park employees who were making repairs found a canoe buried in the spring bed near the Abyss. They moved it to the main building as part of a display on the Native Americans nearby. Since that day, women have reported a beautiful Indigenous woman who appears in the bathroom. She sometimes plays with stall doors while giggling. Other times, she walks inside the bathroom, says something in a language they can't understand, and then runs toward the wall. She goes straight through and vanishes before their eyes, her words echoing all around them.

Morris Died of a Broken Heart

Ocala

Have you ever gone to see a play in the theater? You probably spent the whole time watching the people on the stage. You may not have noticed the people working the lights. You probably did not spend time wondering who made the costumes or painted the sets. If the play was good, it's likely that you were totally focused on the story, transported to a different time and place. But it takes many people to put a show together. From the actors to the directors to the people who control the sound, they work as a team. They spend hours together and form a close bond. The theater has a long history, and part of it has to do with ghosts and superstitions.

For example, you are never supposed to whistle in a theater, even if there is no show happening. Some say it is to avoid waking the dead. The ghosts of deceased actors who once performed there might be watching. If they do not like it, they might make things go wrong.

The word *Macbeth* must also never be spoken in a theater. *Macbeth* is a famous play by William Shakespeare. There is said to be a curse on the play. If you say the name of the play, the story goes, bad things will happen during the production.

One of the most important traditions in the theater is to always leave one light on when you leave, usually either onstage or pointing toward it. This is so any ghosts who came in can find their way out.

Apparently, a man named Morris Osborn did not have this on his mind as he was building his theater in Ocala. He would do something no one had ever done before. There would be no ghosts of past productions. There would be no curses or dead actors jealous that they could not be part of the show. There would only be magic. There would only be *Morris*.

Morris had wanted to be a famous magician his whole life. He had tried other jobs, but his mind always came back to being in front of an audience. He wanted to see the look in their eyes as he made something disappear and hear them cheering in amazement as he brought it back. Even when Morris moved away from Florida, he knew he would be back. In the 1940s, he returned to his native Florida with his new wife, Kay. They worked all kinds of jobs, including working with animals at Silver Springs. Morris practiced and performed magic as much as he could. His skills improved. He even invented special devices called the Acrobatic Thimbles and the Third Hand. Magicians still use these today. But Morris knew he needed his own theater to do his act right.

Morris bought some land in Ocala. He did not have a lot of money to build his theater, so

he used the cheapest materials he could find. To save on the cost, he often cut corners on the construction. Everything was designed around the show that he wanted to produce. There was special lighting to fit his tricks. He had a trap door installed so his assistant could fall through it. He even built odd angles into the design so the audience could not sit in places where they would see his secret movements. It took some time, but his theater was finally finished. Morris got ready for his first show.

For only $1.25, people were allowed to enter the Morris Osborn After-Dinner Theater and see his first magic show. He called it *The Girl from Nowhere*. That night, the audience fell in love. Morris performed each trick perfectly. Dressed like a fancy wizard, he made them *ooh* and *aah* time and again. Morris was elated. The night had been a huge success. All of his planning had worked.

The next day, people in the town talked all about Morris and his magic. You just had to see his show. A few nights later, he went on again. The theater was packed. He did the same tricks. Each one was perfect. But to his surprise, the audience did not seem to be enjoying it as much as they had on the first night. They applauded, but there were no cheers. Some people became bored and left before the show was over. When it was done, Morris felt like he had failed.

A week later, Morris suffered a heart attack and died. But those who knew him said he'd died of a broken heart. People in town even started to whisper that he had died on stage. His wife was sad when she had no choice but to sell the theatre to the Marion Players, who eventually renamed it Ocala Civic Theatre. The theater fell into terrible disrepair. At times, the curtains moved because of all the rats behind them. The sound was terrible. The bathrooms were close to the stage and the audience would hear the toilets flush during performances. Everything creaked and moaned. But still, the people loved going to the theater. It was not perfect, but it was theirs.

Morris loved it, too. His ghost was a regular there. The actors onstage would see him sitting in the rafters watching them. Empty chairs would suddenly fold down as if someone had taken a seat. Morris really liked sitting in the back. No one was allowed in while the plays were in rehearsal, but Morris was there. If an actor missed a cue, Morris would turn all the lights out. He knew performances needed to be perfect. The audience was picky. If someone working the lights during the show messed up, Morris helped them. He would turn on the spotlight at the right time. He would also lower the lights to help with the mood.

Directors said Morris would also change things. If they had made a mark on the script that Morris didn't like, they would soon find the script scrunched up in a ball. When directors were deciding which actor or actress to cast in a play, Morris would move his choice's picture to the top of the pile.

People who worked at the theatre got used to him. He would play with their keys. He would bang on the wall to remind them to turn out the lights. Once, Morris locked all the doors in the theater. Someone had been trying to take the ticket sales money, and Morris made sure he could not escape. Some said they could hear a voice running lines on the stage even when they were alone in the theater.

Morris's ghost could not scare the rats away. He could not make the building safe or change the weird way it had been built. After a few years, Morris's theater became offices and then was torn down.

The theater company moved to a new location, hoping that Morris would come along with them. But Morris has not shown up to change the lighting or make suggestions about the cast. It seems he may have moved on and given up on his dream of becoming a famous magician or hearing the cherished sound of applause. Perhaps he'll find his way there someday. After all, a magic trick is best when you do not see it coming.

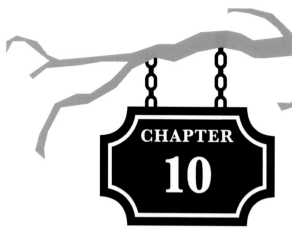

CHAPTER 10

Dark Bunker, Shadow Man

PALATKA

Shadows are only scary at night. In the dark of your bedroom, you see something that looks like a man watching you from the corner. Outside, you hear something pass by your window as you try to sleep. You throw off your covers and turn on the lights, ready to fight these monsters. Luckily, once your eyes adjust, you realize the creepy shadows were nothing but a pile of clothes and toys you forgot to put away. You sigh with relief and turn the lights back off. Yet even then, you are left wondering if maybe the monster was just hiding. Now, imagine you see the shadow of a man. He's standing right near you. Even though you can't see any face or eyes, you know he is looking at you. And the sun is still out.

This creepy feeling is bad enough when you are safe in your home, but imagine when you are alone, out in the middle of a desolate forest, doing one of your favorite activities such as geocaching. Geocaching is a fun hobby that lets you search all over for secret hidden treasures. Some are in plain sight. Others are hidden in the woods or underneath big stones. You can get an app for your phone that tells you where they all are. When you find one, you mark on your account to show that you were there. Most times, you also pick up something someone has left for you and leave something for the next person. But this can be a dangerous thing in the Ocala National Forest.

In the town of Palatka, there is a geocache sight known as The Bunker. It marks an old cement structure about ten feet high. There are many bunkers like this throughout the forest. No one quite knows what they are for. Some believe they were once used for military training. Others think they might be left over from some work that was being done in the forest.

The Bunker is set off about fifty feet into the woods. There is a road nearby, but most people travel in the area using dirt bikes and off-road vehicles. You would not be able to see The Bunker if you were not looking for it. The cement is covered in slimy moss. You can't get to the top unless you have a ladder or stand on someone's shoulders. Once on the top, you can see an entrance to the bottom. You have to use a rusty broken staircase to get to it. The bottom is usually flooded because of the swamp and the rain. It is the kind of place you should never go to. The ghost there usually keeps most people away.

Allen was trying to find it one day. He was an experienced geocacher who had found most of the places in the area. The Bunker took him years to locate. In addition to being dangerous, it also disappears sometimes. This might sound impossible, but it's just the kind of spooky thing that often happens in and around Ocala National Forest.

Allen had heard other people had found The Bunker. They had marked it on their maps and taken pictures next to it. It should have been easy to locate, but every time Allen got nearby, his GPS would go out. It would just spin or send him in the wrong direction. Now, he wishes he had stopped trying.

"It took me years, but I decided to go with my gut. My app had stopped helping me again. I knew it was only a few hundred feet away, so I walked in the direction I thought it was. I got the feeling I was being watched."

Allen could see something large in the woods. He assumed it was The Bunker and started toward it.

"A dark figure ran from it. The sun was starting to set, but it was still light. There shouldn't have been shadows. I had my flashlight, just in case, and tried to follow him with it. He was gone. The whole time I was there, I kept seeing him. I'm telling you, there was enough light for me to see if it was a real person."

Whatever it was would make a sound on

one side of The Bunker. Then it would appear on the other side. It was impossible. Allen was getting scared and tired. He decided to leave.

"He was just standing there in my way," Allen said. "No face, nothing. But I could tell he was staring at me. I ran and ran but could not get back to the road. I could hear him breaking branches behind me. He was chasing me, and I could not get out."

When Allen finally got to the road, it was dark. There weren't even any stars in the sky. Allen had spent only a few minutes at The Bunker. But when he checked his watch, more than two hours had passed.

Barbara found The Bunker while she  was doing a little mudding in the area: driving an all-terrain vehicle. It was midday, and she was paying attention to the road when a man suddenly appeared out of nowhere. Oddly, when she got out to look for him, he was gone.

He was a featureless shadow wearing an old-time hat pushed down one side of his face. "Then I heard a moan from the woods. I thought maybe I knocked him into the trees."

Barbara was seeing what so many others had before. He looks like thick, dark smoke but in the form of a man. Sometimes, he is solid and even makes footprints in the mud. Other times, people say if they reached out to touch him, their hands would go through him. Of course, no one ever tries to touch him. His hat is part of the shadow, felt more than seen. When witnesses try to describe him, even they seem confused. No one can exactly say what they saw.

The voice Barabara heard was coming from the woods. She followed it, ready to help him if he was hurt. After a few minutes, she came across The Bunker.

"That thing in the road was sitting on it. He was cross-legged and looking in my direction. There were no eyes. It was just this dark thing in the shape of a man with no face." Barbara

ran back to her car and drove away. It was years before she told anyone what happened to her.

To this day, she is not sure what she saw. She reads that other people have experienced the same thing.

People still do not know who the man may be or why he seems to be guarding The Bunker. They just know it's best to keep your distance. You decide to hunt for treasure somewhere else. Maybe someplace where there are no shadows.

A Ghostly Goodbye

You've heard the stories. Ocala National Forest is about the experience. There is no way to fully understand it. I know you have questions. They probably don't have answers. Generations have been asking them. For more than a hundred years, people have asked if the Stiniki are real. They have asked what those lights in the trees are, and why ghostly children wander the roads at night. They have asked who that man is leaning against a tree before disappearing like smoke.

Did you imagine seeing him? Was he a strange trick of the light . . . or something much more sinister?

The answers are not important. Moments don't need to have meaning. Instead, share these stories with people you know. Notice how they react when you talk. Sometimes they will not believe you. Other times, they will not *want* to believe you. That is how you can notice a true ghost story. It feels like it could be true, even if it doesn't make sense.

You have now become part of the story.

Chistopher Balzano is a writer, researcher, folklorist, and current host of the podcast Tripping on Legends. He has been documenting the unexplained since 1994 and has been a figure in the paranormal world through his book, articles, and his work as the director of Massachusetts Paranormal Crossroads and now Tripping on Legends (www.trippingonlegends.com). He's the author of *Haunted Ocala National Forest* and several other spooky books.

Check out some of the other *Spooky America* titles available now!

Spooky America was adapted from the creeptastic *Haunted America* series for adults. *Haunted America* explores historical haunts in cities and regions across America. Here's more from the original *Haunted Ocala National Forest* author, Christopher Balzano: